PILGRIMS
IN AMERICA

By L. L. Owens

Content Advisor:
Richard J. Bell
History Department
Harvard University

Rourke
Publishing LLC
Vero Beach, Florida 32964

www.rourkepublishing.com

Image Credits:
Library of Congress, cover (top left and right), 2, 4, 6, 8–9, 10, 11 (top), 15, 16, 18, 19, 20–21, 22, 24, 25, 27 (bottom), 28, 30, 31, 32–33, 35, 37, 39, 40, 41, 43 (bottom), 44, 45 (top and bottom), 46 (first, second, fourth, fifth in first column, all on second column); North Wind Picture Archives, cover (bottom right), Photodisc© 8, 9; Stock Montage, 12–13, 17, 36, 43 (top), 45 (second of column), 46 (second of first column); iStockphoto, cover (bottom left), 5, 7, 11, 27 (top)

Editorial Direction: Red Line Editorial, Inc.; Bob Temple

Editor: Nadia Higgins

Designer: Lindaanne Donohoe

Fact Research: Laurie Kahn

Library of Congress Cataloging-in-Publication Data

Owens, L. L.
  Pilgrims and Puritans / by L.L. Owens.
      p. cm. — (Events in American history)
  Includes bibliographical references and index.
  ISBN 1–60044–122–X (hardcover)
  ISBN 978-1-60044-354-1 (paperback)
 1. Pilgrims (New Plymouth Colony)—Juvenile literature. 2. Puritans—Massachusetts—History—17th century—Juvenile literature. 3. Massachusetts—History—New Plymouth, 1620–1691—Juvenile literature.
 I. Title.

  F68.O94 2007
  974.4'02—dc22

                                                     2006018723

Rourke

Publishing LLC
Vero Beach, Florida 32964

Table of Contents

Chapter One

Harvest Feast of Thanksgiving

I n October 1621, the Pilgrims hosted a historic feast. They had landed at Plymouth, Massachusetts, just about one year earlier after a long, difficult sea voyage from England. Since then, they had built their first homes, planted their first crops, and learned to communicate with the native people of the land. The Pilgrims had settled a new American colony. It was time to celebrate.

Plymouth was the second permanent English colony in America. The first, in Jamestown, Virginia, had been settled in 1607.

People of the First Light

The Wampanoag Indians lived for thousands of years by the coasts of modern-day Massachusetts and Rhode Island. Their tribal name means "People of the East." It also means "People of the First Light," because the sun rises in the east.

The Wampanoag lived in villages. Their homes were bark-covered huts called wigwams. They fished, planted corn and other crops, and hunted wild game. Some of the more interesting animals they hunted included pigeon, bear, moose, raccoon, skunk, and squirrel. They preserved food through traditional methods of drying and smoking.

When the Pilgrims arrived in 1620, the Wampanoag had recently suffered some major losses to their population. Many Wampanoag had died due to war and disease.

The Pilgrims started their settlement at a former Wampanoag village called Pawtuxet. The Indians had abandoned the village a few years earlier during a plague that was spread, unintentionally, by European fishermen.

Some of the remaining Wampanoag helped the Pilgrims by teaching them how to farm the land and survive the harsh seasons. The Wampanoag people of today work to preserve their cultural heritage. They share their own stories of what life was like when the Pilgrims arrived in America.

Autumn had brought fields full of fresh, ripe vegetables. Plymouth governor William Bradford decided to do something special in honor of the colony's first good harvest. He wanted the Pilgrims to give thanks to God for their successful settlement. He declared that there would be a great feast. He invited Chief Massasoit and the rest of the native Wampanoag tribe. Ninety Wampanoag Indians joined the 50 or so Pilgrims for a huge three-day celebration.

Plymouth governor William Bradford welcomes Wampanoag Chief Massasoit to the Pilgrims' first harvest feast.

The harvest was plentiful, so the Pilgrims knew they would have enough food to last through the coming winter. Although there are just two known eyewitness accounts of this feast of thanksgiving, we do know a few details.

They served freshly caught fowl such as swan, duck, and goose. Their tables were also filled with wild fruits and berries. Vegetables such as corn, cabbage, carrots, cucumbers, radishes, turnips, onions, and beets made a colorful display.

"Many [Pilgrims] afterwards [wrote] so largely of their plenty here to their friends in England, which were not feigned but true reports."

Plymouth governor William Bradford Of Plymouth Plantation, 1620–1647

The Wampanoag added food to the celebration, too. They offered their Pilgrim friends fish, clams, lobsters, oysters, five deer, and several wild turkeys.

Many people think the Pilgrims' feast of 1621 turned into the annual Thanksgiving celebration Americans observe today. In fact, the Pilgrims did not even hold a similar celebration the very next year. It would be another 242 years before Thanksgiving would become an official national holiday.

Above: Wild turkeys like the ones served at the first Thanskgiving
Right: The Pilgrims and Indians shared food and friendship at the harvest feast of October 1621.
Next page: A white-tailed deer like the ones hunted by the Wampanoag Indians

"[The Wampanoag] went out and killed five deer, which they brought to the plantation and bestowed on our governor, and upon the captain and others."

Pilgrim Edward Winslow, Mourt's Relation: A Journal of the Pilgrims at Plymouth, 1622

Over the years, several U.S. presidents declared a one-time national Thanksgiving day. General George Washington did in 1777, for example. And New York established an annual statewide Thanksgiving celebration in 1817.

Thanksgiving Day was finally declared a permanent national holiday by Abraham Lincoln, the sixteenth president of the United States. On October 3, 1863, he issued a Thanksgiving Proclamation, setting the holiday on the last Thursday in November. It is thought that he chose this time frame to correspond with the Pilgrims' landing at Cape Cod, Massachusetts, on November 21, 1620.

Above: George Washington
Left: Abraham Lincoln

"I do therefore invite my fellow citizens . . . to set apart and observe the last Thursday of November next, as a day of Thanksgiving and Praise."

President Abraham Lincoln, Thanksgiving Proclamation, October 3, 1863

In 1939, President Franklin D. Roosevelt proposed that the holiday be changed to fall on the fourth Thursday in November. The idea was to give people—and businesses—more time between the Thanksgiving and Christmas holidays. Congress approved the change in 1941. Americans have stuck to that date ever since.

Franklin D. Roosevelt

Almost 250 years after the Pilgrims' feast, Thanksgiving became the official holiday Americans observe today.

Chapter Two

Who Were the Pilgrims?

Who were the Pilgrims, and why did they want to travel to America in the first place? The word *pilgrim* refers to a person who travels to a holy place. The term also is commonly used to describe a small group of English Puritans who left England in search of religious freedom. These Puritans were called Separatists. Their goal was to break away, or separate, from England's national religion, the Church of England.

Separatists did not use the term *Pilgrims* to describe themselves. It wasn't commonly used until around 1669, when writers started referring to the Pilgrim Fathers in articles about the *Mayflower* and the settlement of Plymouth, Massachusetts.

The larger group known as the Puritans wanted to change, or purify, the Church of England. They felt the religion placed too much importance on its leaders and not enough on the teachings of the Bible. Puritans lived by strict rules. They believed in hard work and dedication to their religion. Many felt that they could not freely practice their religion in England.

Separatists took the Puritan view even further by wanting to start their own religion. That was looked down upon by others in their country. Separatists did not believe in having one national religion. They believed people had a right to form local churches that could be governed individually, based on the beliefs of the members of each church. So they journeyed to America to start a new colony. They hoped to live and worship—and build whole communities—according to their beliefs.

"They [Separatists] could not long continue in any peaceable condition, but were hunted and persecuted on every side."

William Bradford
Of Plymouth Plantation, 1620–1647

"Some were taken and clapped up in prison, others had their houses beset and watched night and day."

William Bradford
Of Plymouth Plantation, 1620–1647

The Separatists sailed to America aboard the *Mayflower*. They made up only about one-third of the 102 passengers on the famous trip. The rest were English people looking for new opportunities in America. To keep things simple, many sources label all those who traveled on the *Mayflower* as Pilgrims.

Some of the Pilgrims had left England to settle in Leiden, Holland, in 1607 and 1608. There they were free to worship as they pleased. But the living conditions were terrible. The adults and children alike worked long hours for very little pay. The older members of the group saw how the children fit into Dutch society by learning the language and spending all their time among the Dutch citizens. The elders worried that the community was losing its own cultural traditions. These Pilgrims felt they could start a new, better life in America. In 1620, they left Holland for England and then continued on across the Atlantic Ocean.

An illustration from 1880 dramatically portrays the Pilgrims boarding a boat to leave Holland.

Pilgrim Occupations

Few Pilgrims had any formal education, and none of them were political figures in England. Most worked hard at humble occupations that they intended to continue once they reached America. Of the 58 men and boys on the *Mayflower*, the trades and occupations of 32 are known. Their jobs included:

blacksmith (one who makes and repairs iron)

camlet maker (weaver of a luxurious cloth)

carpenter

cooper (one who makes and repairs wooden barrels)

cordwainer (one who makes shoes and other items from soft leather)

hatter (one who makes hats)

merchant (a store owner)

physician

sailor

salter (one who sells salt and/or treats food with salt to preserve it)

sawyer (one who saws wood)

servant

silk worker

soldier

tailor (one who makes and repairs clothes)

tanner (one who turns animal skins into leather)

teacher

weaver

wool comber (one who prepares wool to be made into cloth)

The Pilgrims made huge sacrifices in order to pursue their dreams of freedom. They had to give up everything familiar in their lives, including their homes, friends and family, and communities. They could take very few of their belongings on the trip, so most sold their possessions to raise money.

With equal parts fear and courage, the Pilgrims were determined to make a new life for themselves. They left their homes knowing that when they got to the New World, they would be without food, shelter, and jobs. Everything would be brand new.

A Pilgrim gathers wood for a fire soon after arriving in America in the winter of 1620.

Pilgrims worked together to build houses in their new colony.

The Pilgrims overcame many hardships. As time passed, future generations of English settlers turned to the Pilgrims' example for hope through difficult times. To many even today, the Pilgrims hold a special place in the country's history. They are a symbol of the American spirit.

For this reason, perhaps, Pilgrims are a familiar image in U.S. culture. When people hear the word *Pilgrims*, they immediately think of serious-looking men with tall black hats, big white collars, and buckled shoes. Or they imagine women wearing long black dresses with white aprons and dark capes.

Pilgrim clothes were not necessarily black-and-white.

A Pilgrim woman always wore a cap or bonnet.

In reality, Pilgrims didn't dress like that. It's true that some of the Pilgrims' clothing was plain black-and-white. But all black was usually saved for Sundays or more formal occasions. Pilgrims regularly wore coats, pants, dresses, and hats in many vibrant colors, including red, green, blue, brown, yellow, and violet.

Pilgrims did not wear buckles on their hats, belts, or shoes. Buckles like the ones commonly associated with the Pilgrims did not come into fashion until later in the century.

A Pilgrim woman usually wore a two-piece wool dress made up of a fitted bodice (the upper part) and a long, buttoned skirt. Sometimes she would add a lace collar and shirt cuffs. When working around the house, she put an apron over her dress. She always wore her long hair pinned up and hidden under a cap or bonnet.

Pilgrim men wore baggy knee-length pants, or breeches, with stockings and flat leather shoes.

Members of a typical Pilgrim family do chores around the kitchen.

On top, they wore a jacket over a linen shirt with a lace collar and cuffs. They also wore a felt hat and a cloak over their jackets.

Pilgrim children—both boys and girls—wore long gowns of wool or linen in a variety of colors. (Blue was most common for children.) They wore these until about age eight, when they would start dressing more like their mothers and fathers.

Chapter Three

On the Mayflower

*T*he Pilgrims' original voyage started from Southampton, England, on August 15, 1620. The group, which was made up of people from both Leiden and London, planned to sail to northern Virginia in America to settle a new colony. The Pilgrims would cross the Atlantic Ocean in two ships—one called the *Speedwell* and another called the *Mayflower*. Both ships were named after flowers.

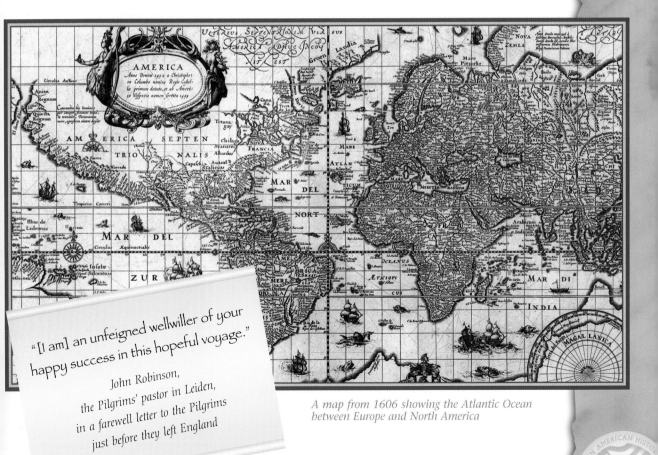

"[I am] an unfeigned wellwiller of your happy success in this hopeful voyage."

John Robinson, the Pilgrims' pastor in Leiden, in a farewell letter to the Pilgrims just before they left England

A map from 1606 showing the Atlantic Ocean between Europe and North America

The *Speedwell* was a small ship. It had already carried some of the Pilgrims from Holland to meet up with the rest of the traveling party in England. The *Mayflower* was much larger than the *Speedwell*. It had been used for years as a trading vessel.

The trip to America had a rocky start. The *Speedwell* was overloaded with people and supplies. Both the *Speedwell* and the *Mayflower* returned to port twice during the next couple of weeks as the captains tried to fix the problem.

When dangerous leaks were discovered in the *Speedwell*, the ship was deemed unseaworthy. It could not make the journey. So some of its passengers crowded onto the *Mayflower*. Not all of them would fit, though. The rest decided to stay in England and travel to America the following year.

Finally, the *Mayflower* left England's Plymouth Harbor on September 16, 1620. It carried 102 passengers and a crew of about 30.

Uncertain of their future, the Pilgrims pray for success before departing for America.

The voyage to America was long and difficult. It took 66 days. During that time, the Pilgrims—and the *Mayflower*—endured several storms. The ship would violently bob at times in the dark, choppy waters of the Atlantic. Horrible bouts of seasickness were common. During the trip, there was one death and one birth.

"They [Pilgrims aboard the *Mayflower*] were encountered many times with cross winds and met with many fierce storms with which the ship was shroudly shaken, and her upper works made very leaky."

William Bradford
Of Plymouth Plantation, 1620–1647

Despite being much larger than the *Speedwell*, the *Mayflower* was considered a small ship. Very little was written about the physical appearance of the *Mayflower*, which was likely built around 15 to 20 years before bringing the Pilgrims to the New World. Based on the measurements of the *Mayflower II*, a replica built in the 1950s, the original ship was probably about 106 feet (32.3 meters) long and 25 feet (7.6 meters) wide.

We do know that the ship itself was damp and dim—it wasn't the most cheerful setting for a long journey. The ship's captain, Christopher Jones, had his own roomy cabin. But all 102 passengers lived in a single room about the size of a modern volleyball court. The room was called the tween deck, and passengers spent most of their time there. That's where they ate, slept—probably in bunks and hammocks—and passed the days away talking about what they would find in the New World.

Above: The Mayflower II *was built to look as much as possible like the original* Mayflower. *Below: Published around 1850, this drawing shows the* Mayflower *surrounded by the ship's tools and equipment.*

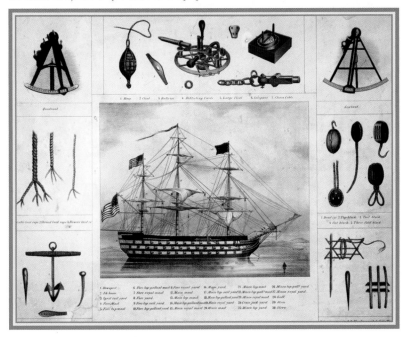

The Mayflower Compact

During the Mayflower voyage, Pilgrims from Leiden and Pilgrims from London found themselves disagreeing about some things. Tensions ran high enough that some of the passengers worried about a possible shipboard mutiny. So the entire group resolved their conflict by reaching an agreement. Its terms were spelled out in the Mayflower Compact. The Pilgrims agreed that on the ship and in the new colony, they would form a government based on majority rule. This meant that when issues came before the group for a vote, the side with the most votes would win.

The 23 female passengers were not allowed to vote. But 41 of the male passengers voted by signing the Mayflower Compact. This happened on November 21, 1620, while the ship was anchored off Cape Cod, Massachusetts.

Some talked about America's vast, thick forests and how they would learn to farm the land. Others shared fears of needing to fight off wild animals and being attacked by native peoples.

> "Having undertaken for the Glory of God . . . and Honour of our King and Country ... a Voyage to plant the first colony in the Northerne Parts of Virginia; do, by these Presents, solemnly and mutually in the Presence of God and one of another, covenant and combine ourselves together into a civill Body Politick. . . ."
>
> *The Mayflower Compact*

Pilgrim men signed the Mayflower Compact *aboard the* Mayflower *on November 21, 1620.*

There was no real privacy on the tween deck. The Pilgrims went up to the main deck only once in a while. It was best for them to stay out of the busy crew's way.

Passengers on the *Mayflower* had few of their personal belongings with them. They had been careful to pack only those things they really needed. These included tools for hunting and building, food, clothing, and some furniture such as tables, chests, and beds. Some were able to take along small collections of books. Many took comfort in their family Bibles.

No one bathed on the ship, and there were no bathrooms. Passengers used chamber pots— or the open sea.

Men did a few chores on the ship, such as cleaning. Women spent the days caring for the 30 children on board and cooking some meals, but most of the cooking was done by the crew.

"They [the Pilgrims] committed themselves to the will of God and resolved to proceed."

William Bradford
Of Plymouth Plantation, 1620-1647

There was no organized school. Children passed the time telling stories, singing songs, and playing games such as *I Spy*. There were few toys. Kids could be found playing with simple cloth puppets and marbles.

Meals were prepared in the crew's quarters. People on the *Mayflower* ate oatmeal, cheese, dried beef and fish, butter, peas, raisins, prunes, fish stew, and "ship biscuits" —hard, twice-cooked bread. The trip lasted longer than they had planned, so the Pilgrims were low on good food by the time the ship reached Plymouth.

Chapter Four

The First Winter at Plymouth

On November 19, 1620, the *Mayflower* encountered a storm that changed the course of history. The Pilgrims had been crossing the Atlantic Ocean bound for the shores of northern Virginia in America.

The storm made it dangerous for the ship to continue sailing in a southwest direction. The *Mayflower* had to alter its route in order to keep its passengers safe. As a result, the Pilgrims ended up at Plymouth.

In this 1846 illustration, Pilgrims row from the Mayflower *to the shores of present-day Massachusetts.*

Pilgrim Leaders

Starting a new life was difficult. The Pilgrims looked to a few strong leaders to help ensure the success of their colony. Names frequently mentioned among Pilgrim leaders include John Carver, William Bradford, Myles Standish, and John Alden.

John Carver was elected Plymouth's first governor at the signing of the Mayflower Compact. He had been a strong presence on board and even before, as he had helped organize the trip from Leiden. Sadly, he died just a few months after arriving at Plymouth. William Bradford was voted in as his replacement. He was elected governor of Plymouth Plantation 30 times in 36 years.

Myles Standish led many of the Pilgrims' early expeditions to explore the Cape Cod area and determine where to settle. While most of the Pilgrims fell ill during that first winter, Standish remained healthy. He helped care for the sick throughout the season.

John Alden was a seaman aboard the *Mayflower*. He quickly became an important member of the colony, though, and was active in its government for many years. Alden was one of the last surviving *Mayflower* passengers. He died in 1687 at around age 88.

On November 21, the ship found a good spot to land on Cape Cod, in what is now Provincetown, Massachusetts. The passengers did some exploring to determine whether they wanted to stay.

A group led by passenger Myles Standish found the supply of fresh water scarce and the soil poor. So the Pilgrims decided to keep going, in search of a better area to settle.

Myles Standish leads a group of Pilgrims through the wilderness. This 1873 illustration is actually depicting a scene from a famous poem about Standish, published by Henry Wadsworth Longfellow in 1858.

On December 21, the *Mayflower* set down its anchor at Plymouth. The Pilgrims were excited to have reached the end of their long journey. But they were fearful of what lay ahead, too.

William Bradford, a *Mayflower* passenger who served as governor of Plymouth Colony almost continuously between 1621 and 1657, wrote about the Pilgrims' early days in the New World. He described the settlers' first thoughts at finally reaching their destination.

"Being thus passed the vast ocean, and a sea of troubles before in their preparation . . . they had now no friends to welcome them, nor inns to entertain or refresh their weather-beaten bodies; no houses or much less towns to repair to."

William Bradford
Of Plymouth Plantation, 1620–1647

Bradford said that people were worried about surviving the coming winter. And they realized all that they had left behind. After such a difficult voyage, they found no friends to greet them as they got off the ship. There were no inns or houses to provide shelter and no meal ready for them when they arrived.

Of the landing and decision to stay at Plymouth, Bradford wrote:

> On Monday they sounded the harbor and found it fit for shipping, and marched into the land and found diverse cornfields and little running brooks, a place (as they supposed) fit for situation. At least it was the best they could find, and the season and their present necessity made them glad to accept of it. So they returned to their ship again with this news to the rest of their people, which did much comfort their hearts.

The Pilgrims were faced with unusually cold, harsh weather during their early days in Plymouth. They had to explore their new land while braving freezing rain and snowstorms. The colonists spent five months living aboard the *Mayflower* while they built their homes. They suffered a few setbacks when two fires broke out at the settlement. The first, in January, destroyed the roof of the first structure the Pilgrims had built. The second, which happened in February, was quickly put out and did little damage.

That winter many Pilgrims lost their lives to the cold, starvation, and illness. By the spring of 1621, just over half of the original 102 *Mayflower* passengers were still alive.

"They that know the winters of that country know them to be sharp and violent and subject to cruel and fierce storms, dangerous to travel to known places, much more to search an unknown coast."

William Bradford
Of Plymouth Plantation, 1620–1647

Pilgrims going to church in the winter

Chapter Five

Plymouth Becomes Home

In February of 1621, the Pilgrims noticed a few American Indians walking near their settlement. This was the first time they had seen any of the native peoples they had feared meeting. They would soon find out if their fears were valid.

Abenaki chief Samoset entered the Plymouth colony on March 16. He greeted a very surprised William Bradford and Myles Standish—in English! Samoset had learned English from hunters, traders, and other early visitors to the area.

"Welcome, Englishmen," Samoset said. The Pilgrims stopped planting their garden to talk to him.

In this painting, American Indians welcome the Pilgrims to their new home. The Pilgrims did not actually meet the Indians for several months.

Samoset was there to gather information for his friend Chief Massasoit, a Wampanoag. He wanted to know whether the Pilgrims would be friends or enemies. To illustrate his question, he showed them two arrows. One was blunt, and the other had a sharp point.

When Samoset was satisfied that the Pilgrims wanted peace, he told them about the plague that had killed the native people who had previously lived on the settlement's land.

On March 22, Samoset visited the colony again with Squanto, an American Indian who also spoke fluent English. Squanto explained that the leader of the Wampanoag, Chief Massasoit, would soon call on the Pilgrims.

Massasoit arrived shortly afterward and exchanged gifts with the colonists. On that day, Massasoit and Plymouth governor John Carver signed a peace treaty. It contained five key conditions:

1. *Indians and Pilgrims would not injure one another.*
2. *Indians and Pilgrims would not steal from one another.*
3. *If one group was unjustly attacked by an enemy, the other group would help them.*
4. *All members of the Wampanoag Nation would honor the treaty.*
5. *Neither group would carry weapons when meeting with the other.*

The treaty was upheld for 50 years.

Wampanoag Chief Massasoit

"[Massasoit is] in his best years, an able body, grave of countenance, and spare of speech."

Edward Winslow
Mourt's Relation: A Journal of the
Pilgrims at Plymouth, 1622

"We have found the Indians . . . very loving. . . . We [can] walk as peaceably and safely in the woods here as in the highways in England."

Edward Winslow
Mourt's Relation: A Journal of the
Pilgrims at Plymouth, 1622

Upon signing a peace treaty, Chief Massasoit hands John Carver a peace pipe as a gesture of friendship.

After the signing, Massasoit made several helpful suggestions to the Pilgrims. He told them how to work the land and that it would be best to plant crops of Indian corn, wheat, barley, and peas in early April.

When spring arrived and the building of the colony was well under way, it was time for the *Mayflower* to return to England. Captain Jones offered passage to anyone who wanted to go home. But all of the surviving Pilgrims chose to stay at the colony they called Plymouth Plantation— their new home. They had worked hard to get there and to make it their own, and they weren't about to give up now.

By winter of 1622, the Plymouth Colony was a permanent village.

What Happened to the Mayflower?

After its historic sea voyage, the *Mayflower* stayed in the harbor for five months while the Pilgrims built homes. It left Plymouth for a return trip to England on April 15, 1621. Captain Christopher Jones used the ship for trading until he died in early 1622.

The last known record of the *Mayflower* is from 1624. The ship was said to be "in ruins." At the time, there was a serious wood shortage in England. Many think it is likely that the *Mayflower*—one of history's most famous ships—was torn down and sold as scrap wood.

In the seventeenth century, it would have been unusual for anyone to reuse parts from the *Mayflower* in other buildings. But there are reports that doors from the ship were identified as part of a barn built around 1624 in Buckinghamshire, England. Whether that's accurate is purely a guess.

Today, tourists at Plymouth, Massachusetts, can visit a replica of the original, called the *Mayflower II*.

The ship set sail on April 15, 1621, with just half of its original crew. (The other half had died during the winter.)

Soon the colonists had blocked off a street and planned plots for their property. Before long, they had built two rows of houses with gardens. On the hill above the colony, they built a platform that held six cannons.

During the summer of 1621, the Wampanoag Indians checked on the Pilgrims. They shared more information about farming the land, and they gave them tips about the best places to hunt and fish in the area. Later, Massasoit and Squanto were captured by the Narragansett tribe. The Pilgrims honored their treaty with the Wampanoag and helped free them.

In November 1621, 35 more Pilgrims arrived from England to join the colony. Over the next several decades, more ships would bring those in search of a better life. The colony slowly grew.

"O beautiful for pilgrim feet
Whose stern impassioned stress
A thoroughfare for freedom beat
Across the wilderness!"
—From "America the Beautiful"

By 1675, Wampanoag Indians saw settlers as a threat to their people. Massasoit's son Metacom was chief now, and he was alarmed that the colonists were taking over too much land. Known to the English as King Philip, Metacom led the Indians in a war that soon spread throughout the region. The Wampanoag almost won what came to be known as King Philip's War. Then Metacom was killed in 1676, and the war ended.

Meanwhile, neighboring towns continued to crop up and grow. Some Pilgrims moved away to these towns. However, for 71 years Plymouth Plantation remained its own colony. It joined the Massachusetts Bay Colony in 1691.

Above: Metacom, son of Massasoit, also known as King Philip by the Pilgrims
Left: An 1883 depiction of English settlers gathering to battle Metacom's army during King Philip's War, 1675–76

Biographies

John Alden (ca. 1599–1687)

Alden was a cooper sent with the Pilgrims by the London merchants who helped finance the *Mayflower's* voyage. One popular legend holds that Alden was the first Pilgrim to set foot on Plymouth Rock, a boulder on the beach by Plymouth Colony. He became a strong leader in the colony.

William Bradford (1590–1657)

Bradford helped organize the Pilgrims' voyage to the New World. He was one of the framers of the Mayflower Compact, and he served as the second governor of Plymouth Colony for 30 one-year terms. Bradford's *Of Plymouth Plantation* is one of the most important eyewitness accounts of the Pilgrims' sea voyage and settlement of Plymouth Colony.

John Carver (1576–1621)

Carver was a wealthy businessman who helped the Pilgrims get financial backing to support their journey. Carver served as the first governor of Plymouth. Before his death in the spring of 1621, he also helped establish a peace treaty with Chief Massasoit.

Massasoit (ca. 1590–1661)

Massasoit was chief of the Wampanoag Indians. He and other members of his tribe taught the Pilgrims many of the skills that helped them survive in the New World. He created a peaceful relationship with the Pilgrims that lasted until he died.

Metacom (ca. 1638–76)

Metacom was Massasoit's son, who took over as chief of the Wampanoag Indians in 1662. Known as King Philip by the English, Metacom feared that colonists were taking over too much Indian land. Metacom waged a war in 1675 that almost succeeded in destroying English settlements in New England. The war ended when Metacom was killed by colonial forces in 1676.

Squanto (?–1622)

Squanto was part of the Pawtuxet tribe that lived in what is now Massachusetts and Rhode Island. He went to live with the Wampanoag Indians in the spring of 1621 and soon became a member of the Plymouth Colony. He spoke fluent English and acted as interpreter for the Pilgrims during their dealings with the Wampanoag.

Myles Standish (ca. 1584–1656)

Standish was a passenger on the *Mayflower* who went on to become military leader of Plymouth Colony. In 1627, he was part of the group in the colony that helped buy out the London investors that had financed the Pilgrims' journey and settlement of Plymouth.

Timeline

September 16, 1620
The *Mayflower* sets sail for the New World carrying 102 Pilgrims.

1620

November 21, 1620
Forty-one Pilgrims sign the Mayflower Compact; the Pilgrims land at what will become Provincetown at Cape Cod.

December 21, 1620
The Pilgrims land at present-day Plymouth, Massachusetts.

March 1621
The Pilgrims and the Wampanoag meet.

April 1621
The *Mayflower* sails back to England.

October 1621
The Pilgrims host a harvest feast of thanksgiving.

1675–76
Wampanoag and colonists wage war over land in King Philip's War.

1691
Plymouth Plantation becomes part of Massachusetts Bay Colony.

October 3, 1863
President Abraham Lincoln gives his Thanksgiving Proclamation.

1863

Glossary

chamber pot (CHAYM-buhr POT)
large bowl used in place of a toilet

colony (KOHL-uh-nee)
a group of people who settle in a distant land while remaining citizens of their original country; also the word for the place they settle

game (GAYM)
wild animals, including birds or fish, that are hunted by people

harbor (HAR-buhr)
part of a body of water near a coast in which ships can safely anchor

harvest (HAR-vihst)
crops gathered during a given season

heritage (HEHR-uh-tihj)
a way of life that passes from one generation to the next within a cultural group

linen (LIHN-un)
light cloth made from the stems of flax plants

mutiny (MYOO-tuh-nee)
rebellion against legal authority by refusing to obey orders and, often, attacking officers, especially aboard a ship

native (NAY-tihv)
originating, or coming from, a certain place

plague (PLAYG)
disease that spreads rapidly and infects and/or kills very large numbers of people

port (PORT)
place by the sea or other waterway where ships and boats can dock and load or unload cargo

Puritan (PYUR-ih-tuhn)
a person who wanted to change the Protestant Church of England in the 1500s and 1600s by having stricter rules and simpler church services

replica (REHP-lih-kuh)
an accurate reproduction of an object

tradition (tra-DISH-uhn)
custom or belief handed down from generation to generation

wigwam (WIG-wawm)
Indian hut made by covering a dome-shaped frame of poles with woven mats or sheets of bark

Further Resources

Web Links

Caleb Johnson's *Mayflower*History.com

www.mayflowerhistory.com

This site includes information about the history of the *Mayflower* and its passengers, links to relevant societies and museums, and several full-text primary sources written by the Pilgrims.

Pilgrim Hall Museum

www.pilgrimhall.org

This site offers a tour of the Pilgrim Hall Museum, which houses major exhibits of Pilgrim possessions.

Books

Brooks, Philip. *The Mayflower Compact*. Compass Point Books, 2004.

Grace, Catherine O'Neill. *1621: A New Look at Thanksgiving*. National Geographic Children's Books, 2001.

Selbo, Jule, and Laura Peters. *Pilgrim Girl: Diary and Recipes of Her First Year in the New World*. Star Publish, 2005.

Index